SOLO PIANO

TEARS OF HOPE

Edited by Heather Slater.
Music processed by Paul Ewers Music Design.
Cover designed by Michael Bell Design.
Cover photograph courtesy of
Davies & Starr/Photographer's Choice/Getty Images.

Order No. SB1014
ISBN 1-59235-147-6

Exclusive Distributors:
Music Sales Corporation
257 Park Avenue South, New York, NY 10010 USA
Music Sales Limited
14-15 Berners Street, London W1T 3LJ England
Music Sales Pty. Limited
120 Rothschild Street, Rosebery, Sydney, NSW 2018, Australia

Printed in the United States of America.

www.musicsales.com

SHAWNEE PRESS
part of The Music Sales Group
London / New York / Paris / Sydney / Copenhagen / Berlin / Madrid / Tokyo

Abide With Me

Composed by William Monk

Amazing Grace

Traditional

Adagietto

From Symphony No.5 in C-Sharp Minor

Composed by Gustav Mahler

Adagio for Strings, Op.11

Composed by Samuel Barber

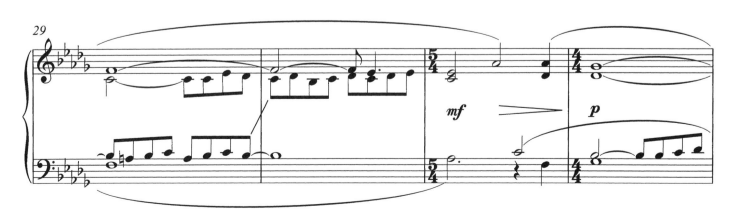

(with increasing intensity)

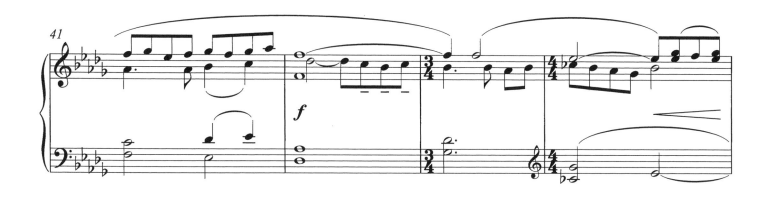

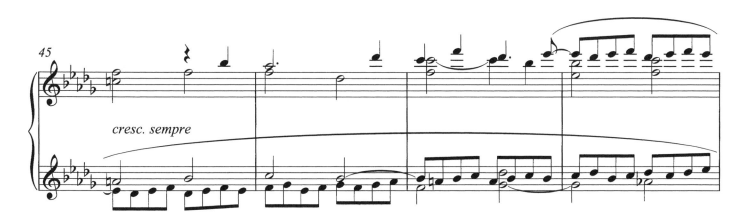

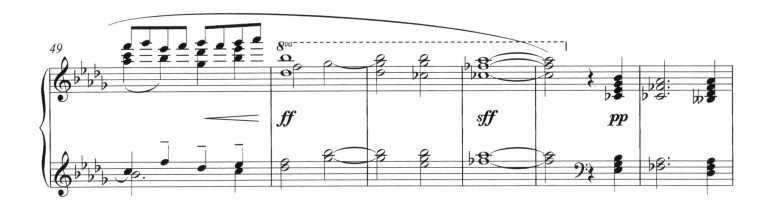

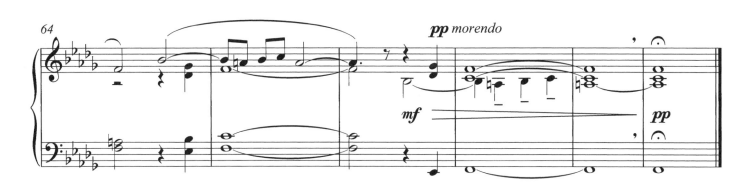

Adagio

Composed by Tomaso Giovanni Albinoni

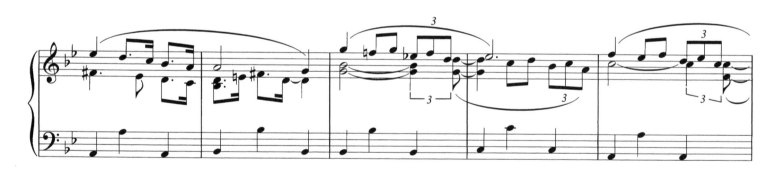

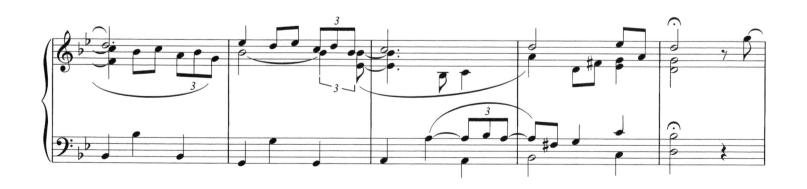

Arioso

Composed by Alessandro Scarlatti

Ave Maria

Composed by Charles Gounod (after J.S. Bach)

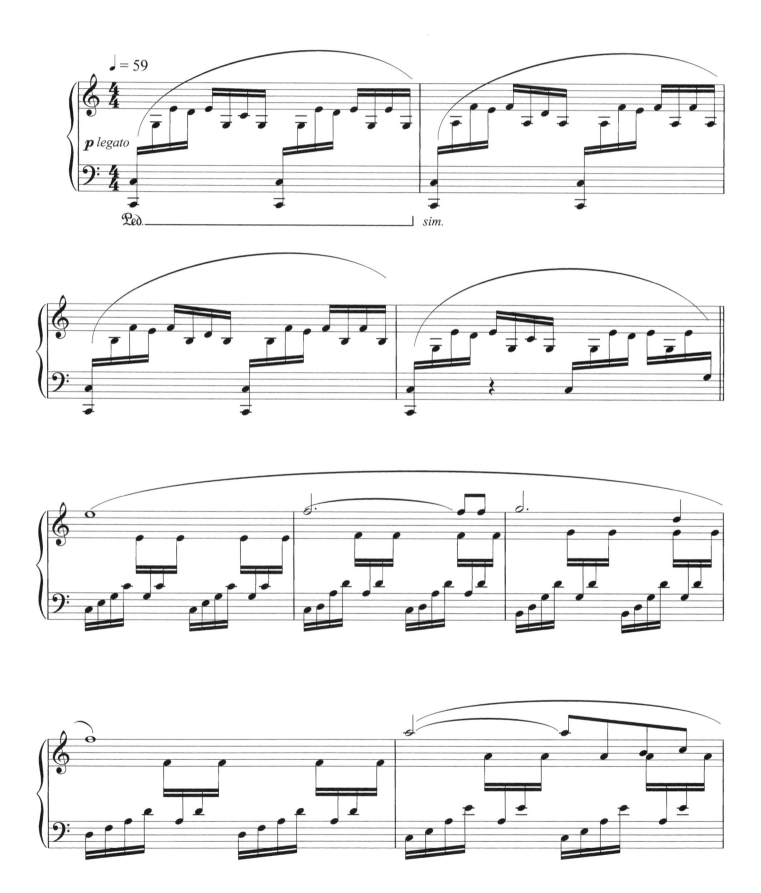

Ave Maria

Composed by Franz Schubert

Ave Verum Corpus, K.618

Composed by Wolfgang Amadeus Mozart

Not too slow

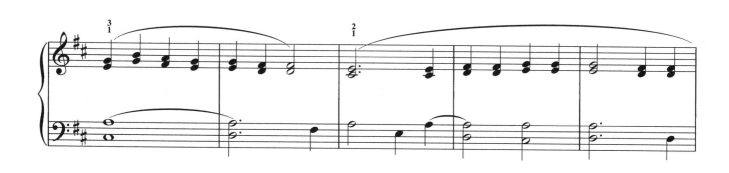

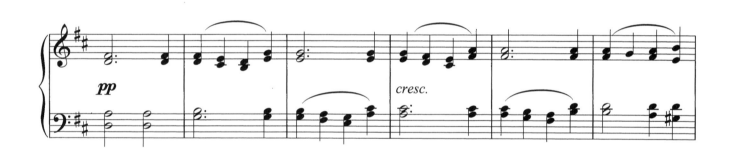

Be Thou With Me

('Bist du bei mir,' BWV 508)

Composed by Johann Sebastian Bach

Andante

Entr'acte from 'Rosamunde'

Composed by Franz Schubert

32

33

Elégie

Composed by Jules Massenet

Lento, ma non troppo

I Would Beside My Lord

From 'St. Matthew Passion'

Composed by Johann Sebastian Bach

I Know That My Redeemer Liveth

From 'Messiah'

Composed by George Frideric Handel

Larghetto

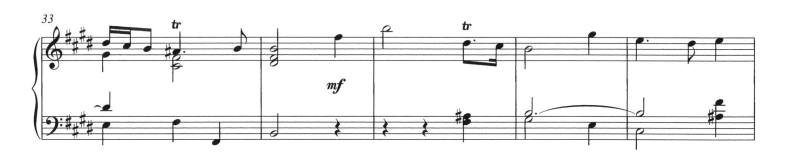

poco rit.

a tempo

In Paradisum

From 'Requiem,' Op.48

Composed by Gabriel Fauré

In Tears Of Grief

From 'St. Matthew Passion'

Composed by Johann Sebastian Bach

Jesu, Joy Of Man's Desiring

Composed by Johann Sebastian Bach

Moderato ♩ = 80

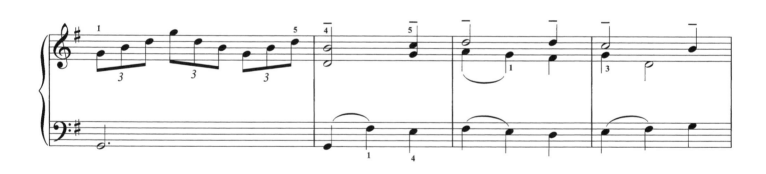

rall. poco a poco

55

Lacrymosa

From 'Requiem,' K.626

Composed by Wolfgang Amadeus Mozart

Largo

From 'Xerxes'

Composed by George Frideric Handel

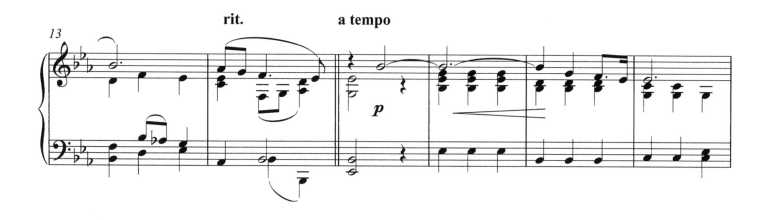

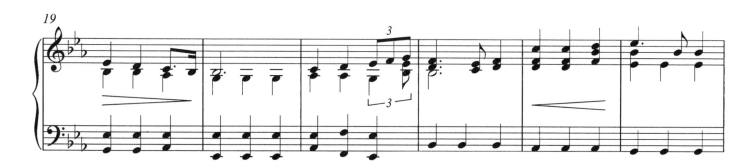

The Lord Is My Shepherd

Traditional (Arranged by Derek Jones)

The Lord's Prayer

Composed by Albert Hay Malotte

Largo

From the 'New World' Symphony

Composed by Antonín Dvořák

Now That The Sun Hath Veil'd His Light

Composed by Henry Purcell

Arranged by Derek Jones

O For The Wings Of A Dove

Composed by Felix Mendelssohn

O Rest In The Lord

From 'Elijah'

Composed by Felix Mendelssohn

Andantino

O Sacred Head Surrounded

From 'St. Matthew Passion'

Composed by Johann Sebastian Bach

Panis Angelicus

Composed by César Franck

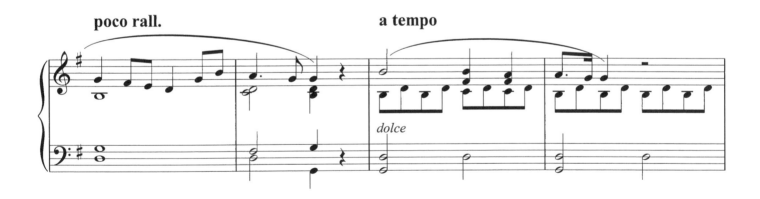

Pavane pour une infante défunte

Composed by Maurice Ravel

Assez doux, mais d'une sonorité large (♩ = 54)

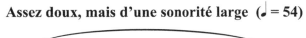

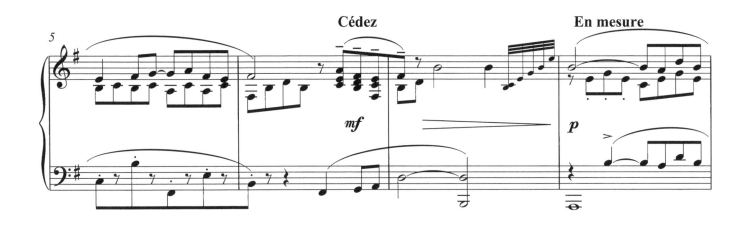

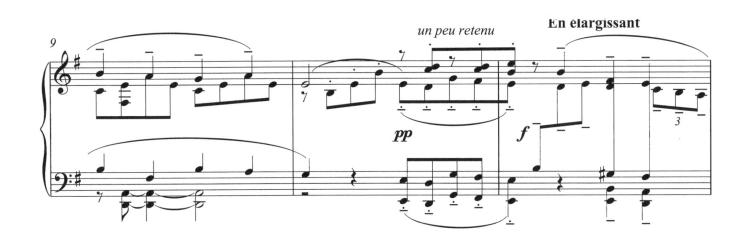

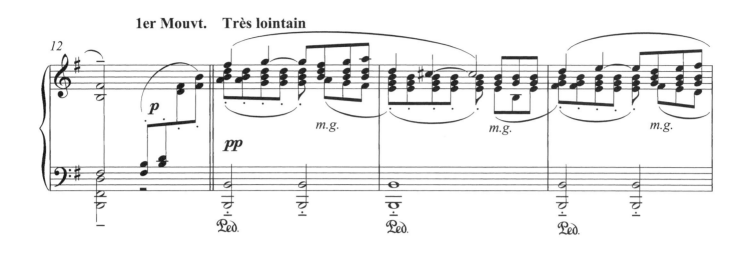

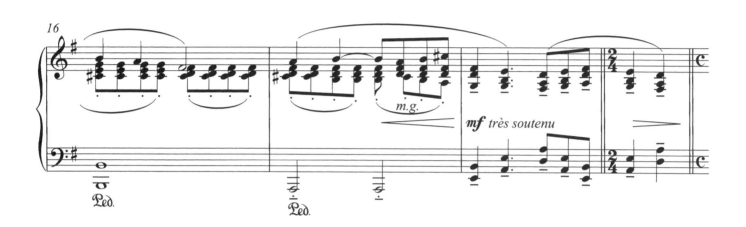

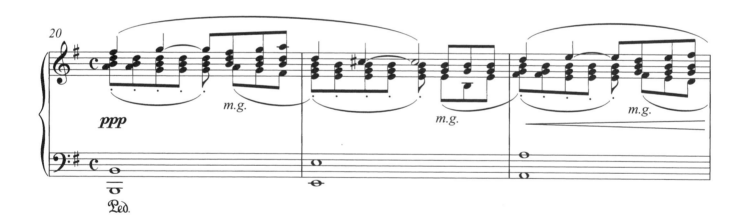

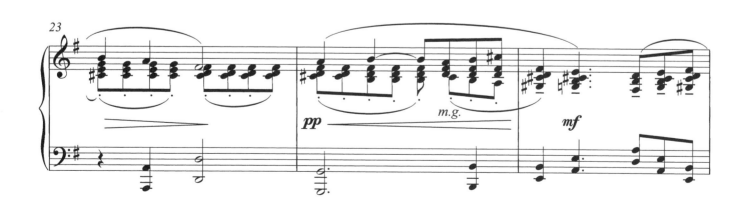

83

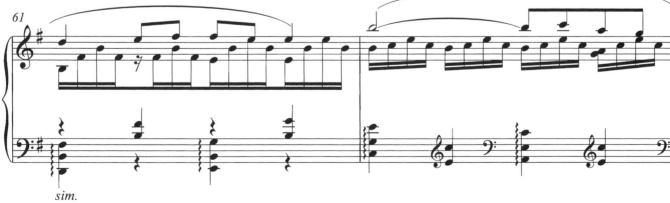

Reprenez le mouvement

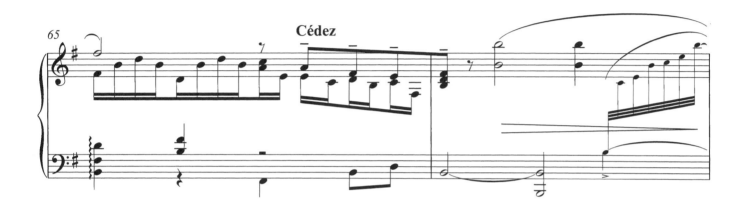

En élargissant beaucoup

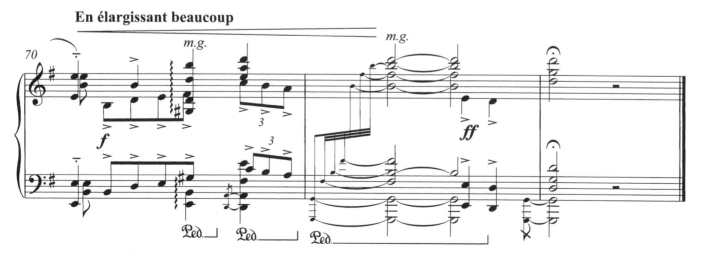

Pie Jesu

From 'Requiem,' Op.48

Composed by Gabriel Fauré

Prayer

Composed by Ludwig van Beethoven

Remembrance

Composed by Robert Schumann

Majestically

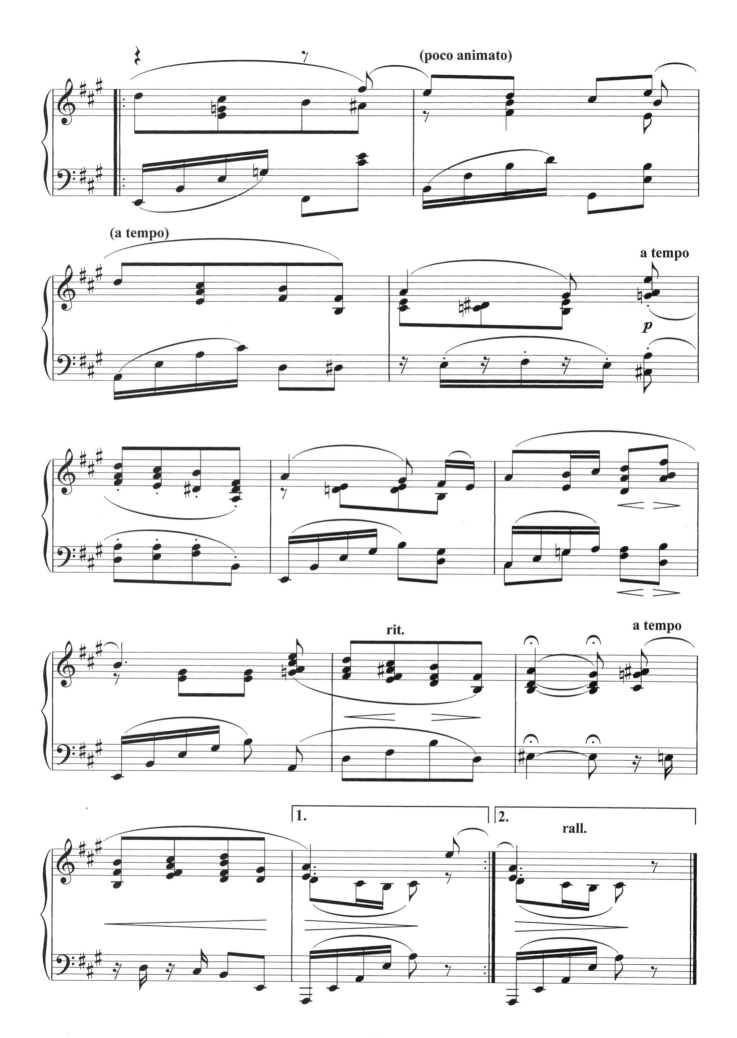

Sheep May Safely Graze

Composed by Johann Sebastian Bach

Prayer

Composed by Carl Maria von Weber

123456789